The Good Ol' Days

Paintings by *Charles Wysocki*

HARVEST HOUSE PUBLISHERS

EUGENE, OREGON

The Good Ol' Days

Text Copyright © 2003 by Harvest House Publishers
Published by Harvest House Publishers
Eugene, OR 97402

Library of Congress Cataloging-in-Publication Data

Wysocki, Charles.
  The good ol' days : paintings / by Charles Wysocki.
    p. cm.
  ISBN 0-7369-1040-9 (alk. paper)
  1. Wysocki, Charles—Themes, motives. 2. Americana in art. 3. Cities and
towns in art. I. Title.
  ND237.W97 A4 2003
  759.13—dc21   2002012042

Design and production by Garborg Design Works, Minneapolis, Minnesota

Harvest House has made every effort to trace the ownership of all poems and quotes. In the event of a questions arising from the use of any poem or quote, we regret any error and will be pleased make the necessary correction in future editions of this book.

Verses marked NIV are taken from the Holy Bible: New International Version®. NIV®. Copyright © 1973, 1978, 1984 by the International Bible Society. Used by permission of Zondervan Publishing House.

Printed in Hong Kong.

03 04 05 06 07 08 09 10 11 12/ NG /10 9 8 7 6 5 4 3 2 1

Memory escapes us. Shapes us. Plays tricks on us like a childhood friend. And it filters our view of today's circumstances through the lens of past events. Lessons we have learned. Stories we can recite the endings to. Dreams we have seen come to fruition. Traditions we have carried with us like priceless heirlooms. Even our most clever, original thoughts are often shiny stones gathered from a riverbed of our past.

Memory molds us. Holds us. And makes us aware of what is important in life. A clear recollection teaches us in a "now" moment and provides us with a proven perspective. A family recipe. A golden oldie.

A tried and true. We didn't knock over milk bottles or guess how many sweets filled the mason jar, yet we claim the grandest prize—memories of the good ol' days.

Most importantly, memories connect us with the values we hold close. The principles we live a good life by. The people we trust and treasure. And memories encourage us to strive for an authentic life. To be proud of our ancestors, our country, our God, and our heritage. Spending time with our memories offers us meaning, identity, and confidence in the connection we have to the cycle of life. It makes our today rich with hope and our tomorrow bright with joy.

Memories of Pumpkin Hill

We called it Pumpkin Hill, for reasons obvious to any observer. It was the backdrop to our family home, and on a sunny autumn morning, the dew glistened and our house resembled a lone package beneath a giant's orange-lit Christmas tree. While I dreamed of pumpkin pies and bread, my little brother had nightmares of the large gourds falling from their vines and tumbling into our house.

Over breakfast, mother would assure him each morning that such a thing has never happened and would never happen. He looked hopeful but still had trouble eating his share of eggs after one of those restless nights. Of course, that could be because once we excused ourselves to take care of chores, I could not resist whispering, "But you never know…" just to watch his eyes grow wide.

When harvest time came, we were both quite excited to earn pocket money by helping Farmer Smith load the pumpkins onto his wagon. Best of all, we were allowed to choose our favorite for carving, and mother received plenty to transform into delicious treats.

I was always a bit sad to see the hill return to a very ordinary, non-threatening mass of green. But as my brother smothered his fresh-baked bread with pumpkin butter, I sensed his relief was as great as his returned appetite.

For the LORD your God will bless you in all your harvest and
in all the work of your hands, and your joy will be complete.

DEUTERONOMY 16:15

To Autumn

Seasons of mists and mellow fruitfulness!
Close bosom-friend of the maturing sun;
Conspiring with him how to load and bless
With fruit the vines that round the thatch-eaves run;
To bend with apples the mossed cottage-trees,
And fill all fruit with ripeness to the core;
To swell the gourd, and plump the hazel shells
With a sweet kernel; to set budding more,
And still more, later flowers for the bees,
Until they think warm days will never cease,
For Summer has o'erbrimmed their clammy cells.

— JOHN KEATS

Love and faithfulness meet together;
righteousness and peace kiss each other.
Faithfulness springs forth from the earth,
and righteousness looks down from heaven.
The Lord will indeed give what is good,
and our land will yield its harvest.
Righteousness goes before him
and prepares the way for his step.

PSALM 85:10-13

Out to Old Aunt Mary's

Wasn't it pleasant, O brother mine,
In those days of the lost sunshine
Of youth—when the Saturday's chores were through,
And the "Sunday's wood" in the kitchen, too,
And we went visiting, "me and you,"
Out to Old Aunt Mary's...

Far fields, bottom-lands, creek-banks—all,
We ranged at will.—Where the waterfall
Laughed all day as it slowly poured
Over the dam by the old mill-ford,
While the tail-race writhed, and the mill-wheel roared—
Out to Old Aunt Mary's...

And then, in the garden—near the side
Where the beehives were and the path was wide,—
The apple-house—like a fairy cell—
With the little square door we knew so well,
And the wealth inside but our tongues could tell—
Out to Old Aunt Mary's.

—James Whitcomb Riley

Memories of Faith

❧❧

In the house of the Lord, the sheep of His flock gather together for song, praise, and worship. Little children sing, "Jesus Loves Me" with twenty enthusiastic, simultaneous, individual renditions. The smudges of syrup and grape juice surrounding their grins are not noticed. The majestic stained glass window centered directly above the young choir members bestows upon them multi-colored halos. For this brief moment, they really are angels.

All rise to sing powerful, moving hymns. Hearts young and old are lifted in the presence of God's blessings and prom-ises. Pastor Smith's message feeds their souls. And after the benediction, Fanny Winston's fried chicken feeds their appetites. No one leaves the churchyard wanting for anything.

Fellowship continues throughout the after-noon. Adults relax and visit under the shade trees while the children play mild versions of their favorite games, avoiding grass stains whenever the thought occurs to them.

Years from now, some children will recall their childhood Sunday school lessons vividly, others will think of the time they hid under the second pew for an entire service, and others still will try to duplicate Franny's batter recipe. And they all will hold tightly to the joy of being a part of one big family.

Surely goodness and love will follow me all the days of my life,
and I will dwell in the house of the LORD forever.

PSALM 23:6

A bit of color against the blue:
Hues of the morning, blue for true,
And red for the kindling light of flame,
And white for a nation's stainless fame.
Oh! fling it forth to the winds afar,
With hope in its every shining star:
Under its folds wherever found,
Thank God, we have freedom's holy ground...

A song for our flag, our country's boast,
That gathers beneath it a mighty host;
Long may it wave o'er the goodly land
We hold in fee 'neath our Father's hand.
For God and liberty evermore
May that banner stand from shore to shore,
Never to those high meanings lost,
Never with alien standards crossed,
But always valiant and pure and true,
Our starry flag: red, white, and blue.

— MARGARET E. SANGSTER

Follow justice and justice alone, so that you may live and possess the land the LORD your God is giving you.

DEUTERONOMY 16:20

The true harvest of my
daily life is somewhat
as intangible and
indescribable as the tints
of morning or evening.
It is a little star-dust
caught, a segment
of the rainbow which
I have clutched.

— HENRY DAVID THOREAU

As Ichabod jogged slowly on his way, his eye, ever open to every symptom of culinary abundance, ranged with delight over the treasures of jolly autumn. On all sides he beheld vast stores of apples; some hanging in oppressive opulence on the trees; some gathered into baskets and barrels for the market; others heaped up in rich piles for the cider-press.

Farther on he beheld great fields of Indian corn, with its golden ears peeping from their leafy coverts, and holding out the promise of cakes and hasty pudding; and the yellow pumpkins lying beneath them, turning up their fair round bellies to the sun, and giving ample prospects of the most luxurious of pies; and anon he passed the fragrant buckwheat fields, breathing the odor of the beehive, and as he beheld them, soft anticipations stole over his mind of dainty slapjacks, well buttered, and garnished with honey or treacle, by the delicate little dimpled hand of Katrina Van Tassel.

— WASHINGTON IRVING
The Legend of Sleepy Hollow

To thee I'll return, overburdened with care;
The heart's dearest solace will smile on me there;
No more from that cottage again will I roam;
Be it ever so humble, there's no place like home.
Home, home, sweet, sweet home!

—JOHN HOWARD PAYNE

There were great changes in my old home. The ragged nests, so long deserted by the rooks, were gone; and the trees were lopped and topped out of their remembered shapes. The garden had run wild, and half the windows of the house were shut up.

It was occupied, but only by a poor lunatic gentleman, and the people who took care of him. He was always sitting at my little window, looking out into the churchyard; and I wondered whether his rambling thoughts ever went upon any of the fancies that used to occupy mine, on the rosy mornings when I peeped out of that same little window in my night-clothes, and saw the sheep quietly feeding in the light of the rising sun.

—CHARLES DICKENS
David Copperfield

Velvet Shoes

Let us walk in the white snow
In a soundless space;
With footsteps quiet and slow,
At a tranquil pace,
Under veils of white lace...

We shall walk through the still town
In a windless peace;
We shall step upon white down,
Upon silver fleece,
Upon softer than these.

We shall walk in velvet shoes:
Wherever we go
Silence will fall like dews
On white silence below.
We shall walk in the snow.

—Elinor Wylie

It came upon a midnight clear,
That glorious song of old,
From angels bending near the earth
To touch their harps of gold:
"Peace on the earth, good-will to men,
From heaven's all-gracious King!"
The world in solemn stillness lay
To hear the angels sing.

—EDMUND H. SEARS

Memories of Father

As I walk through my father's bookstore, his employees wave to me from their rolltop desks. They know me as much by my father's walk as my shock of red hair. I haven't been around these folks since I left for seminary training four years ago. At that time, they all still worked as reporters under my father's editorship at the *Town Chronicle*...before his recent "retirement."

Memories of my reading Scripture passages and fire-n-brimstone sermons from atop the news desk make me cringe a little. As a lad, I thought I was saving these cigar-chompin', rough-talkin' folks. Of course, they were really saving me...a young, nervous boy who surely could not find such a patient, practice flock anywhere else.

Through a maze of dusty volumes, I walk to Father's open office door. Used to watching my father spew commands while proofing copy, berating reporters, and interrogating sources, I am startled to find him reading, silently, at his desk.

Once his eyes register who fills his doorway, he stands to give me a quick but firm embrace. We spend the afternoon talking about the book business and the preaching business. His evident pride in my return to our home church as head pastor touches me. He promises to even catch a few of my sermons. "In case they need editing," he laughs.

The insurmountable differences I focused on as a child now seem non-existent. Sitting here as an adult—among my father's greatest treasure, the written word—I realize Father taught me to be passionate about truth. We do not share the same pulpit, but finally I can see we share the same heart.

For we are the same things our fathers have been;
We see the same sights our fathers have seen;
We drink the same stream, we feel the same sun,
And run the same course our fathers have run.

— WILLIAM KNOX

A long hill ran down to the cove in front of the farm, skirting the rock on the one side and the wood on the other, as already related; every fine evening and every Sunday, all the winter through, this was the chosen toboggan-slope of all the young sledgers of the village.

Eyvind was lord of the slope and owned two sledges "Spanker" and "Galloper"; the latter he lent to larger parties, the former he steered himself with Marit on his lap. At this season, the first thing Eyvind did when he woke was to look out and see whether it was thawing; and if he saw a grey veil lying over the bushes on the other side of the cove, or if he heard the roof dripping, he was as slow over his dressing as if there was nothing to do that day.

But if he awoke, especially on Sundays, to crackling cold and clear weather, best clothes and no work, only catechism or church in the forenoon, and then the whole afternoon and evening free, hurrah! then the boy jumped out of bed with one bound, dressed as if the house were

on fire, and could scarcely eat any breakfast. The moment it was afternoon and the first boy came on his snow-shoes along the roadside, swinging his staff over his head and shouting so that the hills around the lake rang again, and then one came down the road on his sledge and then another and another— straightway off shot the boy on his "Spanker" down the whole length of the slope, landing amongst the late comers with a long, shrill shout, which was re-echoed from ridge to ridge along the cove, until it died away in the far distance.

— BJÖRNSTJERNE BJÖRNSON
A Happy Boy

23

Dashing thro' the snow in a one-horse open sleigh,
O'er the fields we go, laughing all the way;
Bells on bob-tail ring, making spirits bright;
What fun it is to ride and sing a sleighing song tonight!

— J. PIERPONT

The whole country glittered with an icy crust, and people went about on a platform of frozen snow, quite above the level of ordinary life. Claude got out Mr. Wheeler's old double sleigh from the mass of heterogeneous objects that had for years lain on top of it, and brought the rusty sleighbells up to the house for Mahailey to scour with brick dust. Now that they had automobiles, most of the farmers had let their old sleighs go to pieces. But the Wheelers always kept everything...

The moon had been up since long before the sun went down, had been hanging pale in the sky most of the afternoon, and now it flooded the snow-terraced land with silver. It was one of those sparkling winter nights when a boy feels that though the world is very big, he himself is bigger; that under the whole crystalline blue sky there is no one quite so warm and sentient as himself, and that all this magnificence is for him. The sleighbells rang out with a kind of musical lightheartedness, as if they were glad to sing again, after the many winters they had hung rusty and dust-choked in the barn.

— WILLA CATHER
One of Ours

Fine old Christmas, with the snowy hair and ruddy face, had done his duty that year in the noblest fashion, and had set off his rich gifts of warmth and color with all the heightening contrast of frost and snow....

There had been singing under the windows after midnight—supernatural singing, Maggie always felt, in spite of [Tom's] contemptuous insistence that the singers were old Patch, the parish clerk, and the rest of the church choir; she trembled with awe when their carolling broke in upon her dreams, and the image of men in fustian clothes was always thrust away by the vision of angels resting on the parted cloud.

The midnight chant had helped as usual to lift the morning above the level of common days; and then there were the smell of hot toast and ale from the kitchen, at the breakfast hour; the favorite anthem, the green boughs, and the short sermon gave the appropriate festal character to the church-going; and aunt and uncle Moss, with all their seven children, were looking like so many reflectors of the bright parlor-fire, when the church-goers came back, stamping the snow from their feet.

—GEORGE ELIOT
The Mill on the Floss

Spring Is Here

When the wisteria's vine begins to flower
Spring is here.
When children beg to play for one more hour
Spring is here.

When colors sprout from the earth and put on a show
Spring is here.
When you plot and plan what your garden will grow
Spring is here.

When you discover you are humming a childhood rhyme
Spring is here.
When hope, like white jasmine, starts its climb
Spring is here.

—HOPE LYDA

The year's at the spring,
And day's at the morn;
Morning's at seven;
The hill-side's dew-pearl'd;

The lark's on the wing;
The snail's on the thorn;
God's in His heaven —
All's right with the world!

—ROBERT BROWNING

Memories of Tradition

Once each spring, my mother hosted her sisters for a quilting party. I greeted each visiting aunt with a kiss on the cheek before retreating to my favorite spot midway up our one flight of stairs. For a shy, preadolescent girl, this was the perfect vantage point to take in the brilliantly colored pieces of fabric and the equally beautiful women in my life.

As they each worked on a quilt, they would sing favorite hymns and talk about their families. I listened to tales about my many cousins, all of them male, with great delight. To keep me involved, my mother had me serve lemonade mid-afternoon. My presence was celebrated with talk of how I had grown into such a pretty young lady. I beamed and blushed under their notice and would shift my attention to their quilts. Each aunt had a unique style in all that she did, and I dreamed of being a bit like each one of them.

As was tradition, at the end of their three-day visit, my aunts created for me a patchwork sundress made from the fabric remnants—a skirt of yellow sunflowers, a border of pink rosebuds, a sash of sky blue. I would wear the annual dress with great pride.

Each spring, my dream of becoming a blend of these women grew stronger. They were clothing me with courage, creativity, and womanhood; they were helping me become who I was meant to be.

What's young women made of?
Rings and jings and all fine things
And that's what young women's made of.

—ANONYMOUS

Old-Time Spelling Bee

Have you noticed the children mumbling around town—
Their lips move silently as they stare at the ground.
Why the strange behavior, soon you will see.
It seems it is time for the Spelling Bee.

"Catastrophic," says Mary, last year's winner,
As she practices the hard words after dinner.
"Fabulous," spells Benjamin, a sharp contender indeed
As he stands in the coop and tosses the feed.

Miss Littleton asks for silence among the schoolhouse crowd
Of parents and siblings so eager and so proud.
She pronounces the next word with a clear voice.
Samuel begins reluctantly, wishing for another choice.

So very close! But he misses by one letter.
Mary approaches the podium, hoping to do better.
She takes her time and starts quite strong.
But in the end, she too is wrong.

Benjamin knows that his prayers have been heard.
His personal motto happens to be this very word.
He must use it in a sentence in order to claim his fame.
"As the youngest of five brothers...
PERSEVERANCE is my middle name."

— HOPE LYDA

And though now I am small and young,
Of judgment weak and feeble tongue,
Yet all great, learned men, like me
Once learned to read their ABC.

— DAVID EVERETT

Memories of Treasures

Only on a Saturday is the chance to enter a barn considered the prelude to fun and not to chores. But not just any barn—only the one at the Peppercricket Farms flea market filled with homemade delights, trinkets, riches, and not-so-obvious heirlooms.

Treasure seekers pause to wave and greet neighbors and friends who have also sought out the promised shade and anticipated adventure of this place. Mrs. Andersen does not notice anyone around her...her eyes focus on the beautiful sugar and creamer set adorned with lilac blossoms and gold trim. She traces each flower with her finger, remembering her mother's similar set—the centerpiece for many afternoon teas. Tears come to her eyes as she recalls how it shattered during the family's move from the farm to town.

The Andersen children rush up to their mother, interrupting the moment of remembering but filling the wake with excitement over their finds: a lopsided wagon, a wood-carved duck, and an illustrated book of nursery rhymes. As Mr. Andersen loads the family into the carriage, Brett, the most observant child, announces, "But father, mother has nothing."

"Don't be silly, child," Mrs. Andersen laughs. "In fact I do have something. Today I take away with me a very special memory. A gift of the heart is the best treasure of all."

"Does that mean you don't want this?" Mr. Andersen smiles as he holds out the delicate floral set to his wife. The children start clapping, and Mrs. Andersen takes in the joy of this moment. The memory of this day will most certainly be counted as a gift for many years to come!

But store up for yourselves treasures in heaven...
For where your treasure is, there your heart will be also.

Matthew 6:20-21

My Lost Youth

Often I think of the beautiful town
That is seated by the sea;
Often in thought go up and down
The pleasant streets of that dear old town,
And my youth comes back to me.
And a verse of a Lapland song
Is haunting my memory still:
"A boy's will is the wind's will,
And the thoughts of youth are long, long thoughts."

...Strange to me now are the forms I meet
When I visit the dear old town;
But the native air is pure and sweet,
And the trees that o'ershadow each well-known street,
As they balance up and down,
Are singing the beautiful song,
Are sighing and whispering still:
"A boy's will is the wind's will,
And the thoughts of youth are long, long thoughts."

— HENRY WADSWORTH LONGFELLOW

Memories of Love

Grandma and Grandpa celebrate their fiftieth wedding anniversary today. Friends and family have traveled to take part in this time of remembering and of rejoicing. The small country church parlor is filled with those who have shared in some part of this couple's journey.

Toast after toast is made in honor of a love that shines more brilliantly with each passing year. Behind each short thank you is a deeper story of Grandma and Grandpa reaching out to neighbors and strangers through labor, loans, and love. Their lives have always been focused on the needs of others; today their eyes are bright and fixed on each other.

I hear stories of how Grandma and Grandpa met; how their union from the very start caused others to say, "They were meant to be together." As a single, young man I watch Grandpa place his arm around his beloved bride, and I witness their love with new eyes. How lucky I am to have such a love modeled for me.

The band plays a favorite song, and we all sing along softly as husband and wife enter the circle and sway together gracefully. They whisper to one another the words that keep them strong, "I love you, dear." And they hold on tightly.

I have loved you with an everlasting love;
I have drawn you with loving-kindness.

JEREMIAH 31:3

And what is so rare as a day in June?
Then, if ever, come perfect days;
Then Heaven tries earth if it be in tune,
And over it softly her warm ear lays...

Now the heart is so full that a drop overfills it,
We are happy now because God wills it;
No matter how barren the past may have been,
'Tis enough for us now that the leaves are green;

We may shut our eyes but we cannot help knowing
...that the river is bluer than the sky.

— JAMES RUSSELL LOWELL

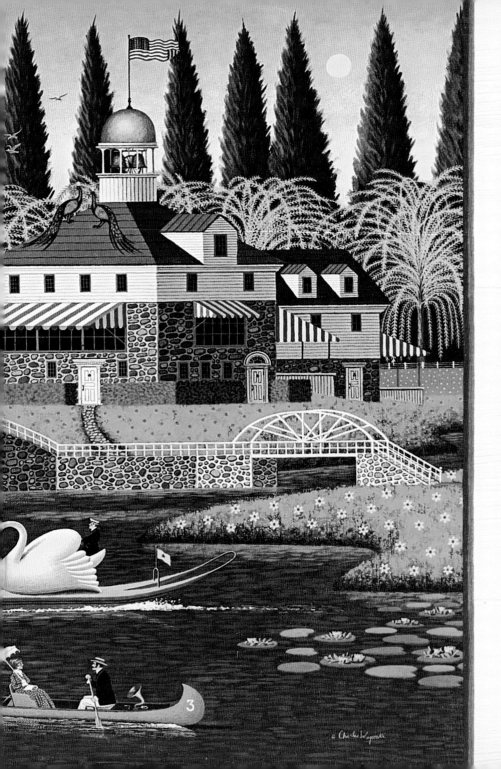

The River of Life

The more we live, more brief appear
Our life's succeeding stages:
A day to childhood seems a year,
And years like passing ages.
The gladsome current of our youth,
Ere passion yet disorders,
Steals lingering like a river smooth
Along its grassy borders.

— THOMAS CAMPBELL

Memories of Country Pride

The Fourth of July parade is about to begin. Places, everyone!

Pastor Smith combs his white beard and tightens his striped vest, regretting the many recent potato casseroles. He will be Uncle Sam because the Missus thought it was the perfect way to represent the love of God and country… so he agreed. Perhaps too hastily, he thinks to himself, reevaluating his wild outfit and his sanity.

Mayor Fredrickson discreetly tries out his new megaphone. It is his third year as Master of Ceremonies. Alexander polishes his triangle and practices his solo. Over and over, Miss Beacham tells the children's marching band to get in formation. She enlists the help of the parents to create a flag out of forty color-coordinated, squirrelly children.

Mrs. Crosby has her basket of freshly made taffy, macaroons, peppermint candies, and chocolate truffles. She will be sure that every child who lines the sidewalk for the big parade receives a treat.

The mayor makes his way to the gazebo. Noticing that everyone is getting restless, he skips to his final remarks, "Together we celebrate one another, this town, and our country. Let freedom ring!" Taking his cue, Alexander plays his triangle with great enthusiasm. Uncle Sam leads the way. Candy flies through the air. The cluster of children resemble a flag. Oh, how everyone loves a parade!

Along the street there comes
A blare of bugles, a ruffle of drums;
And loyal hearts are beating high:
Hats off!
The flag is passing by!

— HENRY HOLCOMB BENNETT

Oh! the old swimmin'-hole! In the long, lazy days
When the humdrum of school made so many run-a-ways,
How pleasant was the journey down the old dusty lane,
Where the tracks of our bare feet was all printed so plain
You could tell by the dent of the heel and the sole
They was lots o' fun on hand at the old swimmin'-hole.

—James Whitcomb Riley

So it's home again, and home again, America for me!
My heart is turning home again, and there I long to be,
In the land of youth and freedom beyond the ocean bars,
Where the air is full of sunlight and the flag is full of stars.

—Henry van Dyke

Memories of Main Street

Every day is a festival when one ventures along Main Street. There is purpose and anticipation in the steps of visitors and towns-folk as they make frequent stops to observe the decorative storefront displays and savor the festive atmosphere. Bright colors, tantalizing scents, and welcoming vendors beckon window shoppers to enjoy a moment or two beyond the awning. An invitation they gladly accept.

Miss Louise hands newcomers sweet truffles from her chocolate shop, Chester the chestnut vendor is generous with his tasty samples and his good cheer, and nobody can pass the dairy cart without Mr. Gilman's story about the origin and wonders of ice cream.

Country folk understand Main Street is one large front porch—a gathering place for neighbors and newcomers. Children, parents, and grandparents nod to one another warmly. Conversations floating above the street like balloons are all about news from kin, the child on the way, and the Sunday social. Family talk.

As the lights are turned off and the vendors close for the evening, young and old couples alike still stroll along the sidewalk. The young twosomes pause momentarily in front of the jeweler's window, dreaming of tomorrow.

The elderly couples walk arm in arm and recall when this very spot was Mr. Appleby's orchard. The cobblestone path becomes a place where the town's history and its future walk side by side.

When all the trading was done, the storekeeper gave Mary and Laura each a piece of candy. They were so astonished and so pleased that they just stood looking at their candies. Then Mary remembered and said, "Thank you."

—LAURA INGALLS WILDER

Shout for joy to the LORD,
all the earth, burst into jubilant song with music.

PSALM 98:4

I Hear America Singing

I hear America singing, the varied carols I hear;
those mechanics—each one singing his, as it should be, blithe and strong;
The carpenter singing his, as he measures his plank or beam,
The mason singing his, as he makes ready for work, or leaves off work;
The boatman singing what belongs to him in his boat—the hatter singing as he stands;
The wood-cutter's song—the ploughboy's, on his way in the morning, or at the noon intermission, or at sundown;
The delicious singing of the mother—or of the young wife at work—or of the girl sewing or washing;
Each singing what belongs to him or her, and to none else;
The day what belongs to the day—at night, the party of young fellows, robust, friendly,
Singing, with open mouths, their strong melodious songs.

— WALT WHITMAN